DATE DUE			

I CAN DO IT!

I CAN USE A COMPUTER

by Susan Ashley

Photographs by Gregg Andersen

Reading consultant: Susan Nations, M.Ed., author/literacy coach/consultant

WEEKLY (WR) READER®
EARLY LEARNING LIBRARY

Please visit our web site at: www.earlyliteracy.cc
For a free color catalog describing Weekly Reader® Early Learning Library's
list of high-quality books, call 1-877-445-5824 (USA) or 1-800-387-3178 (Canada).
Weekly Reader® Early Learning Library's fax: (414) 336-0164.

Library of Congress Cataloging-in-Publication Data

Ashley, Susan.
    I can use a computer / by Susan Ashley.
      p. cm. — (I can do it!)
    Includes bibliographical references and index.
    ISBN 0-8368-4325-8 (lib. bdg.)
    ISBN 0-8368-4332-0 (softcover)
    1. Computers—Juvenile literature. I. Title. II. I can do it! (Milwaukee, Wis.)
  QA76.23.A83   2004
  004—dc22   2004043762

This edition first published in 2005 by
Weekly Reader® Early Learning Library
330 West Olive Street, Suite 100
Milwaukee, WI 53212 USA

Copyright © 2005 by Weekly Reader® Early Learning Library

Editor: JoAnn Early Macken
Graphic Designer: Melissa Valuch
Art Director: Tammy West
Picture Researcher: Diane Laska-Swanke
Photographer: Gregg Andersen

Printed in the United States of America

2 3 4 5 6 7 8 9 10 09 08 07 06

Note to Educators and Parents

Reading is such an exciting adventure for young children! They are beginning to integrate their oral language skills with written language. To encourage children along the path to early literacy, books must be colorful, engaging, and interesting; they should invite the young reader to explore both the print and the pictures.

I Can Do It! is a new series designed to help young readers learn how ordinary children reach everyday goals. Each book describes a different task that any child can be proud to accomplish.

Each book is specially designed to support the young reader in the reading process. The familiar topics are appealing to young children and invite them to read — and re-read — again and again. The full-color photographs and enhanced text further support the student during the reading process.

In addition to serving as wonderful picture books in schools, libraries, homes, and other places where children learn to love reading, these books are specifically intended to be read within an instructional guided reading group. This small group setting allows beginning readers to work with a fluent adult model as they make meaning from the text. After children develop fluency with the text and content, the book can be read independently. Children and adults alike will find these books supportive, engaging, and fun!

— Susan Nations, M.Ed., author, literacy coach,
and consultant in literacy development

I can use a computer.
I can play games on
the computer.

This is the monitor.
I see pictures and
words on the monitor.

monitor

I type on the keyboard. The keys have letters and numbers. Some keys have words.

keys

This is the mouse.
I **click** the mouse
with my finger. I
press down and
let go.

I use the mouse to move the pointer in the window. The pointer looks like an arrow.

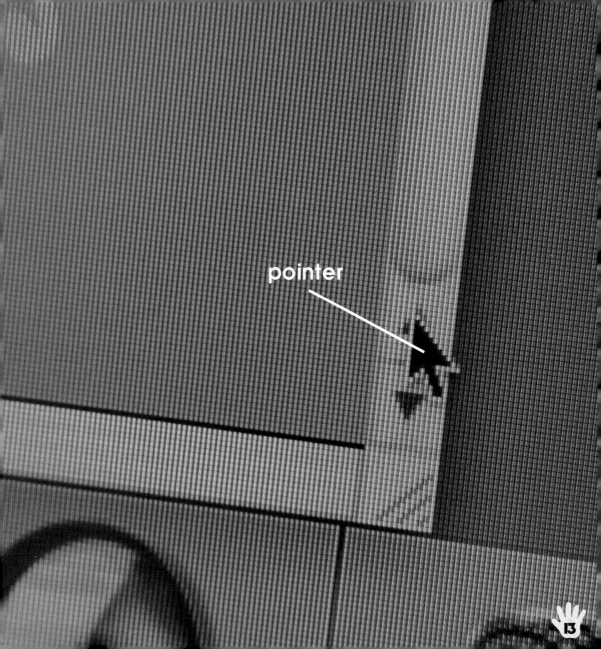

pointer

I can click a picture or a word. I click a picture to start a game.

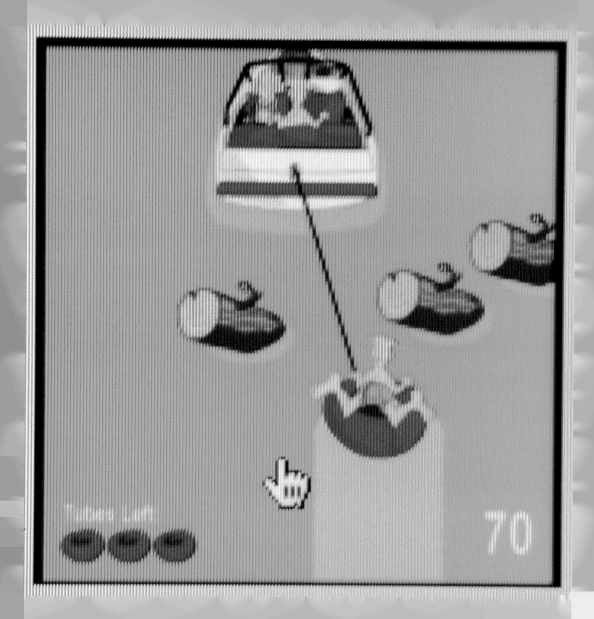

Clicking can open a new window. I can scroll to see the whole window.

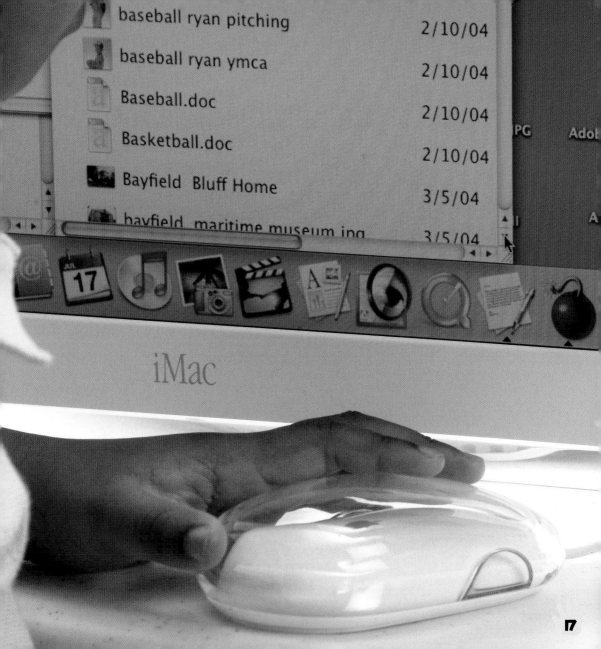

baseball ryan pitching   2/10/04

baseball ryan ymca   2/10/04

Baseball.doc   2/10/04

Basketball.doc   2/10/04

Bayfield Bluff Home   3/5/04

bayfield maritime museum.jpg   3/5/04

PG   Adob

iMac

There are words at the top of the window. I click the word "Back" to go back.

about:blank

Back   Forward   Stop   Refresh   H

Address: @ http://games.funschool.com/game

@ Live Home Page   @ Apple   @ Apple Support

Games and Activi

Game FAQs   Game Guide

Bobber's Farm

Playing games on the computer is fun. Learning on the computer is fun.

Glossary

keyboard — a set of keys used for typing

monitor — the part of a computer that shows pictures and words. The monitor looks like a TV screen.

mouse — a small device that moves the pointer. Moving a mouse lets you do many things on the computer.

pointer — an arrow that points to things in a window

scroll — to move things in a window up or down

window — an area on the monitor that can be opened and closed

For More Information

Books

Computers. Catherine Chambers (Heinemann Library)

I Like Computers: What Can I Be? Muriel L. Dubois (Bridgestone Books)

Safety on the Internet. Lucia Raatma (Capstone Press)

Using Computers: Machine with a Mouse. Math Monsters (series). John Burstein (Weekly Reader Early Learning Library)

Web Sites

World Almanac for Kids Online
www.worldalmanacforkids.com
Play games, explore, and learn cool facts about almost anything

Index

About the Author

Susan Ashley has written more than twenty-five books for children. She has lived all over the United States and in Europe. Thanks to her travels, she has become very good at reading maps and writing letters. She also likes making — and eating — sandwiches. Susan lives in Wisconsin with her husband and two cats. The cats like it when she makes tuna sandwiches!